Divine Healing in the Atonement

Divine Healing in the Atonement

Paul Brewster

SUNESIS MINISTRIES LTD

Divine Healing in the Atonement

Copyright © 2018 Paul Brewster. The right of Paul Brewster to be identified as author of this work has been asserted by him in accordance with the Copyright, Designs, and Patents Act 1988. All rights reserved. No part of this publication may be reproduced or transmitted in any form or by any means, electronic or mechanical, including photocopy, recording, or any information storage and retrieval system, without permission in writing from the author.

ISBN 978-0-9956837-6-1

Published by Sunesis Ministries Ltd. For more information about Sunesis Ministries Ltd, please visit:

www.stuartpattico.com

Unless otherwise indicated, Bible quotations are from the Holy Bible, King James Version. Scripture quotations marked "Amplified Bible" are taken from the Amplified Bible, Copyright © 1954, 1958, 1962, 1964, 1965, 1987 by The Lockman Foundation. Used by permission. (www.Lockman.org).

The author of this book does not dispense medical advice or prescribe the use of any technique as a form of treatment for physical, emotional, or medical problems without the advice of a physician, either directly or indirectly. The intent of the author is only to offer information of a general nature to help you in your quest for emotional and spiritual well-being. In the event you use any of the information in this book for yourself, the author and publisher assume no responsibility for your actions.

The views expressed in this book are solely those of the author and do not necessarily reflect the views of the publisher, and the publisher hereby disclaims any responsibility for them.

Contents

Introduction	8
The Fall of Man	10
Divine Healing in the Mosaic Law	16
Divine Healing in Messianic Prophecy	21
The Healing Ministry of Jesus Christ	27
The Healing Ministry of the Christian Believer: Part 1	31
The Healing Ministry of the Believer: Part 2	36
The Hearing of Faith and Healing	40
Faith and Healing	46
Prayer and Healing	53
Generational Curses and Divine Healing	59
God's Medicine For Divine Healing	64
Paul's Thorn in the Flesh	71
Bibliography	78

I dedicate this book to Pastor Curry Blake, General Overseer of John G Lake Ministries who has been an inspiration to this generation and to me, concerning the uncompromising biblical truth about Divine Healing. May God continue to richly bless him in his spiritual endeavours to remove man made traditions from human minds and equip the body of Christ for the last days ministry of the saints.

I also acknowledge and thank my wife, Lorraine for all her help and support in the ministry over the years.

Introduction

Divine healing has become a controversial topic within Christian circles, with a variety of different viewpoints. Some Christians believe it is not always God's will to heal, while others think that healing ceased to exist when the last apostle died. There are also those who believe that sickness is a blessing from God to teach us something, whereas others believe it is Paul's 'thorn in the flesh' to keep a person humble. Conversely, there is a small minority of Christians who have concluded that God is always willing to heal His people.

Many arrive at different conclusions for various reasons; some were taught these views within their Christian denominations. Others came to their own conclusions by their own experiences and observations in life. Amidst the varying views and concepts, we wear them like glasses when we read and interpret what the Bible says about this topic. To one degree or another, we interpret Scripture within the context of our presuppositions, biases and prejudices. These attitudes do have a tendency to adulterate our perceptions even when confronted with the plain truth and meaning of what the Word of God has said. Because of certain issues we have embraced on the journey of life, they have somewhat darkened our mental approach to the infallible Word of God.

The purpose of this book is to honestly attempt to disconnect yourself from your preconceived ideas and biases and seek the unadulterated truth accordingly, as the Apostle Paul said:

"But have renounced the hidden things of dishonesty, not walking in craftiness, nor handling the word of God deceitfully; but by manifestation of the truth commending ourselves to every man's conscience in the sight of God" (2 Cor. 4:2).

As you read this book, seek out the truth prayerfully and honestly as you apply the principles of Scripture interpretation of which "...in the mouth of two or three witnesses every word may be established" (Matt. 18:16), since every true, believing Christian accepts the bible as their rule of faith and standard for practice. May the God of lights open your understanding to His wisdom (Eph. 1:17-18).

1

The Fall of Man

"Wherefore as by one man sin entered into the world, and death by sin; and so death passed upon all men, for that all have sinned" (Rom. 5:12).

Every sickness, disease, death and destruction can be traced back to a cause. To understand the nature of what is going on now, you must comprehend how it began. In order to appreciate God's solution, you must recognise the nature of the problem, or else you will misinterpret the challenges of life as being normal and purposed by God to make you a better person. When Jesus answered the question of the religious leaders about divorce, He went back to "the beginning", the "Bereshit", the Hebrew name for the Book of Genesis (Matt. 19:3-6). Similarly, to find out God's perfect will for life and health, read Genesis 1 and 2 regarding His original plan for health as well as marriage, employment, family, dominion, prosperity etc.

When God finished creating all things, including man, He saw that it was very good (Gen. 1:31). As long as man was in harmony with God, the created order was in harmony with him. The

The Fall of Man

conditions prior to the fall was righteousness, peace, abundance, life and dominion. There was no death or decay, no sickness, disease or pain, no lack or poverty - for the earth yielded her strength. Even the animal kingdom was subservient to him. However, to maintain this utopia, man had to remain submitted to God's will which was this:

"...Of every tree of the garden thou mayest freely eat: But of the tree of the knowledge of good and evil, thou mayest not eat of it: for in the day that thou eatest thereof thou shalt surely die" (Gen. 2:16-17).

Death as a consequence for disobedience would be two-dimensional: spiritual and physical. Spiritually, man died in his spirit to God and the things of God; spiritual life was absent and his fellowship with the Source of life was cut off, thus manifesting itself morally and ethically as sins and trespasses. Ephesians 2:1 states,

"And you hath he quickened, who were dead in trespasses and sins."

This inward spiritual death is what Jesus alluded to when one of His disciples asked to go and bury his father; He said, "...Let the dead bury their dead..." (Lk. 9:60). Because of the sin of Adam, the opening passage of scripture tells us that death passed upon all men (Rom. 5:12). That death is spiritual, ethical and moral, where all who come into this world are born with a sinful and corrupt nature inside. King David declares,

"Behold, I was shapen in iniquity; and in sin did my mother conceive me...The wicked are estranged from the womb: they go astray as soon as they be born, speaking lies" (Ps. 51:5; 58:3).

Even from the womb, we are estranged from fellowship with God because we have inherited the consequences of Adam's sin, of which spiritual death is one, and for that reason, all have sinned. Therefore, we have all committed sins because it was in our nature to do so.

The second aspect of death is the physical. After Adam sinned, God pronounced the consequences for his disobedience, of which physical death was specifically announced,

"In the sweat of thy face shalt thou eat bread, till thou return unto the ground; for out of it wast thou taken: for dust thou art, and unto dust shalt thou return" (Gen. 3:19).

Physical death is the separation of the spirit and body, whereby the spirit returns to God who gave it (Eccl. 12:7) and the body returns to the dust of the ground (Eccl. 12:7; Gen. 2:7; 3:19). God never created man to die but to have eternal life as a unity: spirit, soul and body (1 Thess. 5:23). When physical death occurs, it interrupts this union. However, the hope of the resurrection will restore this union on that last day (Jn. 5:25, 28-29; 6:39; 1 Thess. 4:13-17).

There are adversities in life that are designed to propel us to physical demise. Some of these are instantaneous, others gradual, which spans days, weeks, months or years. These calamitous conditions and events come under the category of death,

The Fall of Man

because of their intentions to steal, kill and destroy (Jn. 10:10). Deuteronomy 27:15-26 lists the moral evils that lead to death and destruction, such as idolatry, dishonouring parental authority, injustice against foreigners, orphans and widows, all manner of sexual uncleanness etc. There are also natural evils mentioned in Deuteronomy 28 such as barrenness, famine, sicknesses, diseases, violence and wars, oppression, slave trade etc. They are the result of disobedience (v16-68). The moral evils and the natural evils are categorised as death, evil and curses (Deut. 30:15, 19).

Sickness, disease and infirmities fall under this category. They are never listed as life, good and blessings, because they are the consequences of the fall of man into sin. It is the law of sowing and reaping. Sin and carnality produce death and corruption, but righteousness and spiritual maturity produce life and peace (Rom. 8:5-6; Gal. 6:7-8). Every seed produces after its own kind.

Sickness, disease and infirmities are designated as death – incipient - death (Deut. 30:15, 19; Rom. 4:19), cursing (Deut. 30:15, 19; Gal. 3:13) and evil (Deut. 30:15; 7:15). The Greek term for "sick" is "kakos" and it literally means "evil". Sickness, disease and infirmity are also called captivity (Job 42:10), bondage (Lk. 13:16), and oppression (Ac. 10:38). They are never described as "blessings" from God to His children. The things that God desires to gives to His children are good and perfect gifts (Lk. 11:11-13; James 1:17).

God is not the proximate source of sickness and disease, but is the source of life, healing and health (1 Cor. 12:4-7, 9; Rom. 8:11; Ac. 10:38). Anytime a passage speaks of God sending or putting sickness and disease upon people, there are two things that need to be considered. Firstly, God has sovereign rule and control over all evil, moral and natural, including sickness and disease, and will use them to fulfil His purpose to judge and punish His enemies or to chastise His people when they go astray (Ex. 15:26; Deut. 7:15; 28:20; 1 Cor. 5:5; 11:23-32; Rev. 9). Secondly, since God created the laws of nature, secondary causes and effects, including His allowance for sin and its consequences to enter His creation, He is held sovereignly responsible for every adverse thing that transpires in creation, such as barrenness (1 Sam. 1:5), dumbness, deafness and blindness (Ex. 4:11). However, the focus in Exodus 4:11 is not that He made the blindness, deafness, or the dumbness, but rather that He made dumb, blind and deaf people; the emphasis is on the creation of people regardless of their disabilities. And if He created them, He could also cure them. This is the message He wanted to make known to Moses so that he would understand that his lack of eloquence was not an issue with God. The same applies to the healing of Hannah's barren womb (1 Sam. 1:5, 10-20).

Although sin has brought sickness, decay and death into this world, in the midst of all this death, decay, corruption and disease, God's surpassing purpose for allowing sin and its effects to enter His world is so that the works of God may be made manifest and Jesus Christ be glorified; a principle conveyed in the story of the man born blind:

"And his disciples asked him, saying, Master, who did sin, this man, or his parents, that he was born blind? Jesus answered, Neither hath this man sinned, nor his parents: but that the works of God should be made manifest in him" (Jn. 9:2-3).

Also in the case of Lazarus' death, his sickness was not unto death but for the glory of God so that the Son of God might be glorified (Jn. 11:4).

Satan is the source of sickness (Job 2:3-7; Ac. 10:38). Nevertheless, whatever the Devil intends for evil, God will turn things around for our good and bring praise and honour to Himself. Although the fall has brought a multitude of diseases into our world, God intends for His surpassing grace and mercy to be made known so that where sin abounds, grace will much more abound (Rom. 5:20). God has done much more in Christ than Satan could ever have done in Adam.

2

Divine Healing in the Mosaic Law

"And the LORD will take away from thee all sickness, and will put none of the evil diseases of Egypt, which thou knowest, upon thee; but will lay them upon all them that hate thee" (Deut. 7:15).

The opening verse of scripture presents an unequivocal statement about God's will concerning the health of His covenant people, Israel. He makes a definite promise, by the hand of Moses, concerning what He will do for His people, and what He will refrain from doing if they obey Him.

The Lord begins the verse by saying that He will take sickness away from the midst of them and also declares that He will not put any diseases upon them. This rules out any erroneous notion that God puts sickness upon His children to teach them something. From the above verse, God promises to do no such thing.

In the first clause of the verse, His promise is to take all sickness away. God's will for Israel was for every sickness to be removed from His people so that they would experience total and continual health throughout their lives. There are two other passages of

Divine Healing in the Mosaic Law

scripture that support this view, so that in the mouth of two or three witnesses, every word may be established (Matt. 18:16).

At the waters of Marah, after Israel's exodus and deliverance from Egypt, God made a promise to His people just prior to the giving of the Law at Mount Sinai; it says,

"...If thou wilt diligently hearken to the voice of the LORD thy God, and wilt do that which is right in his sight, and wilt give ear to his commandments, and keep all his statutes, I will put none of these diseases upon thee, which I have brought upon the Egyptians: for I am the LORD that healeth thee". (Ex. 15:26).

The passage, here, presents the condition to walking in, not divine healing, but divine health, whereby no sickness or disease will be able to touch your physical body. Whereas with divine healing, sinners and heathens have been healed from infirmities due to the goodness and mercy of God, that did not necessarily mean that they stayed healed (1 Kgs. 13:4-6; 2 Kgs. 5; Ps. 105:37; Matt. 11:20-24; Jn. 5:6-14; Lk. 11:24-26). To walk in divine health will require you to be obedient to His Word and to appropriate by faith the promise of divine health. The condition is emphasised four times, and the promise is mentioned once. Obedience is the major and the promise is the minor (Ex. 15:26; Prov. 4:20-22).

Then, God sanctions the promise of divine health with His Name: "I am the LORD that healeth thee." This clause is translated from God's Hebrew Name which is His Covenant and redemptive Name in the Old Testament. That Name is "Yahweh Ropheka" and it means the Lord that heals you or the Lord your physician. It is one of His compound names by which He combines a promise to His personal Name "Yahweh." His personal Name "Yahweh" is derived from the Hebrew verb "to be", which depicts His eternal, unchanging nature and character, revealed to Moses at the burning bush, who called Himself "I am that I am" (Ex. 3:14).

So when God attaches a promise to His personal name, like healing, He is saying that it is always in His nature and character to heal, and it has been unchanging in His character to do so. His Name "I am", describes Him to be eternal and unchanging – He was, He is, and shall always be the Healer and Physician. This absolutely obliterates the premise that healing no longer occurs.

What these two passages of scripture (Deut. 7:15; Ex. 15:26) teach us is that sicknesses, diseases and infirmities do not belong to the children of God but to the citizens of Egypt: a type of the ungodly world system ruled over by Satan. It is not the inheritance of children of God to experience sickness, disease and infirmity, for these are of the Devil (Ac. 10:38; Lk. 13:11, 16). Since the people of God do not belong to the world system, that also means that no sickness, disease or infirmity belongs to God's children. Psalm 105:37 reads,

"He brought them forth also with silver and gold: and there was not one feeble person among their tribe."

There was not one person of the children of Israel who was sick, weak or feeble.

The other similar passage of scripture is in Exodus 23:25-26 and it states,

Divine Healing in the Mosaic Law

"And ye shall serve the LORD thy God, and he shall bless thy bread, and thy water; and I will take sickness away from the midst of thee. There shall nothing cast their young, nor be barren, in thy land: the number of thy days I will fulfil."

The verse begins with the exhortation to serve the Lord your God, and in serving Him, He promises to bless your bread and water, and to take sickness away from the midst of you. The same blessing, promised to Israel under the Old Covenant, is also for the New Covenant believer: a Covenant that is far better than the Old and established upon better promises (Heb. 8:6). Moreover, He will even bless what we eat and drink so that there is nothing harmful or deadly in what we consume (1 Tim. 4:3-5). The healing of the bitter waters of Marah is a vivid example of this (Ex. 15:23-26).

Furthermore, the following clause intimates: "There shall nothing cast their young, nor be barren, in thy land..." Nothing casting their young, denotes that there will be no miscarriage of the young which includes humans and animal livestock (Deut. 7:14-15). But there will be fruitfulness and increase in the land. In the New Testament, the godly women do have the promise and assurance of being saved in childbearing: that is, delivered or protected from any physical complications relating to conception, pregnancy or giving birth (1 Tim. 2:15). Also, He promised that there will be no barrenness among His people – male and female - their livestock and agricultural produce (Deut. 7:14; 28:4-5).

In the next clause of this verse, it reads: "...the number of thy days I will fulfil" (Ex. 23:26c). God desires to fulfil the number of your days, and He does this by giving you longevity. In fact, it is not God's will for the life of His people to be cut short due to sickness, disease or some other fatal adversity. He wants His people to live out the number of their days, fulfilling the purpose for which they were born so that when they leave this earth, they leave satisfied and fulfilled. God's promise to us in Psalm 91 is that He will satisfy us with long life which includes a quality of life: health, strength, prosperity, joy, peace and contentment (v15).

3

Divine Healing in Messianic Prophecy

"Surely he hath borne our griefs, and carried our sorrows: yet we did esteem him stricken, smitten of God and afflicted. But he was wounded for our transgressions, he was bruised for our iniquities: the chastisement of our peace was upon him; and with his stripes we are healed" (Is. 53:4-5).

It is important to note that the Old Testament is saturated with Messianic prophecies about His birth, His life, his work and ministry, His death and resurrection, His second coming and more; because they are central to the revelation of the Law and the Prophets. To this, Jesus intimated when addressing His Jewish opponents:

"Search the scriptures: for in them ye think ye have eternal life: and they are they which testify of me... For had ye believed Moses, ye would have believed me: for he wrote of me. But if ye believe not his writings, how shall ye believe my words" (Jn. 5:39, 46-47)?

After Christ's resurrection, He expounded to His disciples the Scriptures concerning Himself (Lk. 24:44-45).

Prophecies in the Old Testament revealed that by Messiah's work, the sick, the blind, the deaf, the lame would be healed, and the dead brought back to life. Hence, the connection between divine healing and the fulfilment of Messianic prophecies. Their fulfilment were to be signs that the Kingdom of God had come. Let us observe some of these prophecies as it relates to divine healing.

In Isaiah 35:4-6 it reads,

"Say to them that are of a fearful heart, Be strong, fear not: behold, you God will come with vengeance, even God with a recompense; he will come and save you. Then the eyes of the blind shall be opened, and the ears of the deaf shall be unstopped. Then shall the lame man leap as an hart, and the tongue of the dumb sing..."

This verse of scripture is a kingdom prophecy that is eschatological and Messianic in nature. It is eschatological because the passage tells us that God will come with vengeance and a recompense, He will come to exact punishment against His enemies; in doing so, He will save His people, Israel, to whom this prophecy was addressed. When God comes, He will come in the person of Messiah. Then the curse that has been upon creation since the fall of man will be removed from the earth under the reign of the King-Messiah so that there will be a thousand years of peace, righteousness, blessings and health, which will result in the blind seeing, the deaf hearing, the dumb singing and the lame walking. This will occur at the second

Divine Healing in Messianic Prophecy

advent of Jesus Christ on a mass scale, of which His first advent was a foretaste of things to come.

At Christ's first coming, He came announcing that the Kingdom of God had come near and demonstrated its presence by healing the sick and the oppressed, casting out devils and raising the dead. Since the Kingdom He announced, and the Kingdom that was to come are one, the miraculous signs He performed in His earthly ministry were a foretaste of the Millennial Kingdom to come. His proclamation at the outset of His ministry was to heal and to set the oppressed free (Lk. 4:17-19; Ac. 10:38), in contrast to the kingdom of darkness whose purpose is to oppress and put in bondage to sickness, disease and infirmities. Where you read about the demon-possessed, you will have to pair it with the sick and diseased (Matt. 8:16-17; Ac. 10:38). Sickness and disease is never a sign of the Messianic Kingdom, it is always presented in Scripture as a sign of the Satanic kingdom. And for this purpose the Son of God was manifested to destroy the works of the Devil (1 Jn. 3:8; Jn. 10:10; Ac. 10:38), even to the point of raising the dead – a precursor of the end time mass resurrection of saints at His second coming (Matt. 11:2-5; Jn. 11:1-45; 1 Thess. 4:14-17). Jesus raising the dead in His earthly ministry was a partial fulfilment of Old Testament prophecies that would eventually culminate at His second advent, referenced in Isaiah 25:8; 26:19 and Daniel 12:2.

And then we come to the monumental passage that is the culmination of all redemptive prophecies: Isaiah 53:4-5,

"Surely he hath borne our griefs and carried our sorrows; yet we did esteem him stricken, smitten of God and afflicted. But he was wounded for our transgressions, he was bruised for our iniquities: the chastisement of our peace was upon him and with his stripes we are healed".

The prophet Isaiah gives the monumental passage on the divine purpose of the suffering Messiah, unparalleled anywhere in Old Testament Scripture. He provides a detailed account of the Messiah's rejection, the substitutionary nature of His sufferings and death, His resurrection and intercession in chapter 53.

What I want to focus on is His substitution as it relates to divine healing. The terms that convey His substitutionary death are the words "borne" and "carried". "Borne" is from the Hebrew rendering "nasa", which means to lift up, to carry, to bear and take away. Its synonym translated as "carried", is the Hebrew word "sabal" and its primary meaning is to bear, to transport; it stresses the process of bearing or transporting a load. Hence, Christ, with these two terms in mind, took our burdens upon Himself and carried them away. According to Isaiah's prophecy, the suffering Messiah was to take our sins, iniquities, griefs and sorrows upon Himself and carry them away.

The terms "griefs" and "sorrows" are from the Hebrew words "holi" and "mak'ob". Holi denotes sickness, disease, illness, and mak'ob signifies pains. Therefore, the suffering servant-Messiah bears and carries away our sicknesses, diseases and pains in the same way He bore and took away our sins and iniquities. So if it is God's will for us is to not have sin, it is also His will for us not to have any sicknesses, diseases of pains in our physical bodies because Jesus has borne them away (Is. 53:4, 6, 11, 12).

Matthew's Gospel quotes verse 4 in context as a fulfilment of Isaiah's prophecy, and it reads,

Divine Healing in Messianic Prophecy

"When the even was come, they brought unto him many that were possessed with devils: and he cast out the spirits with his word, and healed all that were sick: That it might be fulfilled which was spoken by Esaias the prophet, saying, Himself took our infirmities and bare our sicknesses" (Matt. 8:16-17).

Matthew's Gospel records the healings that Jesus performed in His earthly ministry - expelling demons from people and healing all the sick, were fulfilling Isaiah 53:4. When He healed all that were oppressed of the Devil (Ac. 10:38), He was fulfilling the prophecy of Isaiah 53:4. You may ask the question: "How is it that Christ fulfilled this prophecy in His healing ministry prior to going to the cross when Isaiah was speaking of His sufferings and death on the cross?"

There are Old Testament prophecies that have a twofold fulfilment: a partial fulfilment, and a complete fulfilment. The healings that Jesus performed in His earthly ministry were a partial fulfilment of Isaiah 53:4. But when He went to the cross, He completely fulfilled it by bearing our sickness and diseases at the cross. Similarly, as Jesus fulfilled Psalm 2:1-2 at His first advent (Ac. 4), he will completely fulfil it at His second advent (Ps. 2). So Jesus did not only fulfil the Isaiah prophecy at the cross, He also fulfilled it in His earthly ministry. His healing ministry, in advance, is a result of the sacrifice of Jesus on the cross because He was the Lamb of God slain from the foundation of the world (1 Peter 1:20; Rev. 13:8), and therefore forms the basis of God declaring the end from the beginning (Is. 46:10; Rom. 4:17).

Jesus Christ also fulfilled the clause in Isaiah 53:5, "...with his stripes we are healed." Isaiah, in his prophecy about the suffering Messiah, uses past tense verbs to predict a future event (v3-5) for the same reason intimated previously - the Lamb of God slain from the foundation of the world. The clause: "...ye are healed" was pointing to the cross; but when the Apostle Peter quotes the same verse, he says, "...by whose stripes ye were healed" (1 Peter 2:24) because he pointed back to the cross which had already happened.

His "stripes" is translated from the Greek word "molops", and it denotes a bruise, a wail, and a wound that sheds blood (Thayer 1977). Its Greek form is singular, and refers to the deadly stroke of divine judgment upon the body of Messiah, by which we were healed. This stroke included His beating, scourging and crucifixion. Our healing has been fulfilled. It is a done deal! So do not wait on God to heal you, He has already done it. It is your responsibility to take authority over that sickness or devil and take your healing by force, for it is yours (Matt. 11:12).

4

The Healing Ministry of Jesus Christ

"How God anointed Jesus of Nazareth with the Holy Ghost and with power: who went about doing good, and healing all that were oppressed of the devil; for God was with him" (Ac. 10:38).

The opening passage encapsulates the ministry of Jesus with respect to healing. It also demonstrates the will of God in healing. Finally, the verse sets forth the contrast between the works of God and the works of the Devil. These are the specific points I want to discuss in this chapter regarding the healing ministry of Jesus.

To reiterate the point mentioned in the previous chapter - Jesus' healing ministry was done in fulfilment of prophecy as He healed all who were oppressed by the Devil (Matt. 8:16-17). The nature and direction of His ministry was not to leave out anybody who needed healing but to minister freely and impartially to as many people who desired Him to do so. There are scriptural references that show this to be the case (Matt. 4:23-24; 8:16-17; 12:15; Lk. 4:40; 6:19). His ministry was characterised by healing all. You will find no place in the Gospels where Jesus refused to heal anyone. Everyone He laid His hands on was healed (Lk. 4:40).

Jesus' healing ministry was the expression of the will of His Father. He said,

"For I came down from heaven, not to do mine own will, but the will of him that sent me" (Jn. 6:38).

When Jesus' disciples asked Him about the cause of a man's blindness from birth, He replied,

"...Neither hath this man sinned, nor his parents, but that the works of God should be made manifest in him. I must work the works of him that sent me, while it is day, the night cometh, when no man can work" (Jn. 9:3-4).

The works of God to which Jesus referred, were, giving sight to the blind, healing the sick, cleansing the lepers, casting out devils and raising the dead. These are the works of God which Jesus came to do (Matt. 11:2-5). And nowhere in the Gospels, did Jesus put sickness or disease upon them to fulfil some hidden purpose of God. Sickness was not included in the works of God. His works were always to heal, deliver and set at liberty (Ac. 10:38; Lk. 4:18).

In fact, Jesus said that the Father who dwelt in Him was doing the works: healing the sick, cleansing the lepers, casting out devils and raising the dead (Jn. 14:10). The source of the healings, in the ministry of Jesus, was the Father. Jesus did not perform any miracle independent of the Father because without Him, he could not have done it. John 5:19-29 attests to this fact:

"Then answered Jesus and said unto them, Verily, verily, I say unto you, The Son can do nothing of himself, but what he seeth the Father do: for what things soever he doeth, these also doeth the Son likewise. For the Father loveth the Son, and sheweth him all things that himself doeth: and he will shew him greater works than these, that ye may marvel."

It may seem surprising how Jesus said that He can do nothing of Himself, given the fact that He was the Son of God. How is it that Jesus said, "The Son can do nothing of Himself"? Well, the key to understanding His statement lies in the mystery of His Incarnation. The Bible reads,

"Who being in the form of God, thought it not robbery to be equal with God. But made himself of no reputation, and took upon himself the form of a servant, and was made in the likeness of men" (Phill. 2:6-7).

The term "form" is from the Greek word "morphe" and it does not indicate in Greek the outward appearance of something, but rather, the nature and essence of a person or thing inseparable to it. In other words, the person or thing could not exist without it; it is the essential core of a person's existence. Hence, Christ existed in the form of God – His essence and nature as invisible Spirit, possessing all the divine attributes of Deity and Godhood.

However, the passage goes on further to read, "But made himself of no reputation..." (v7a); in the Greek it says, "But he emptied himself". The clauses following this explain its meaning: "...and took upon himself the form of a servant, and was made in the likeness of men". He emptied Himself by taking the frailty of our humanity upon Himself, thus laying aside the independent use of His Divine attributes of omnipotence, omniscience and omnipresence. Therefore, as a man, the Son of God could do nothing of Himself but was reliant upon the Father and His Spirit to aid Him in doing the work of the ministry.

Although He was God, He was also man, and therefore needed to function on the earth as a man anointed with the Holy Spirit and power to heal all who were sick and oppressed by the Devil (Ac. 10:38; Lk. 4:18-19). Because of this, Jesus' ministry becomes an example and model for all His followers and removes any excuse as to why we cannot walk as Jesus walked. The same Spirit that worked in Jesus of Nazareth is now living in you (Rom. 8:11; 1 Cor. 3:16; 6:19). You can do the same things as He did for you have become a partaker of His divine nature by the new birth, and the Gift of the Holy Spirit and power has been made available to you (Lk. 24:49; Ac. 1:4-5, 8).

What Jesus saw His Father do – the miracles and healings – was the result of Christ doing the work of the ministry. The Father worked as Jesus Himself was also working, for God was doing the works through Him. Therefore, Christ, in not doing the works on His own, set the stage for His ministry of healing to be an example for His disciples.

5

The Healing Ministry of the Christian Believer: Part 1

"Verily, verily, I say unto you, He that believeth on me, the works that I do shall he do also; and greater works than these shall he do; because I go unto my Father" (Jn. 14:12).

Jesus presents a very profound promise for every believer to walk in. It is prefaced with "verily, verily", indicating that what He was about to say was profound, amazing and surpassing the extraordinary. The preface is a double annunciation used in Hebraic expression signifying something deep, profound and superlative – the maximum or highest level of description (Is. 26:3). I will now go on to explore this verse in this chapter.

Jesus states that the key to walking in the healing ministry of Jesus is to believe on Him. Faith is what unlocks the supernatural power of God in mighty works. "Believing on Me" is having faith that Jesus is the Christ, the Son of the living God – the means by which one is saved or born again (Jn. 3:16-18; 1 Jn. 5:11).

The second aspect to believing on Jesus Christ is that you are promised the gift of the Holy Spirit as an enduement of power as was spoken by Christ's own lips:

"In the last day, that great day of the feast, Jesus stood and cried, saying, If any man thirst, let him come unto me, and drink. He that believeth on me, as the Scripture hath said, out of his belly shall flow rivers of living water. But this spake he of the Spirit, which they that believe on him should receive: for the Holy Ghost was not yet given; because that Jesus was not yet glorified" (Jn. 7:37-39).

Those who believed on Jesus as the Saviour and Baptiser in the Holy Spirit would receive the Spirit as Rivers of living water flowing out of their innermost being. By this, they are empowered to do the works of Jesus as He did in His earthly ministry. The same Spirit that was in Christ is also given to His disciples to do the same works that He did (Ac. 1:8; 2:1-4). Hence, the statement,

"...he that believeth on me, the works that I do, shall he do also..." (v12).

The works of Jesus spoken of here, is in the present tense, which indicates that Christ is continuously and repeatedly doing His miraculous works of healing the sick, raising the dead and casting out devils. Christ has not stopped working; the supernatural signs and gifts of the Spirit are for today (1 Cor. 12-14; Mk. 16:17-20; Heb. 2:3-4). How is He doing His works? He is doing them through His believing disciples to whom He has given authority and power to do His supernatural acts of healing. The Gospel of Mark chapter 16:17-18 reads,

"And these signs shall follow them that believe: In my name shall they cast out devils, they shall speak with new tongues; they shall take up serpents; and if they drink any deadly thing, it shall not hurt them; they shall lay hands on the sick, and they shall recover."

These supernatural signs and miracles will follow those who believe in His Name as they followed Jesus in His earthly ministry (Ac. 2:22). We are called to do the supernatural works that He did (Jn. 10:32, 37-38). Christ's works were signs that He was the Son of God; the works that we do in His Name are designed to confirm that same message.

John 14:12 not only tells us that we shall do the works of Christ, but that we will do greater works than these because he goes to the Father. Firstly, I have heard it taught that the believing disciples will do greater works than Jesus Christ. This is foreign to the teachings of the New Testament for two basic reasons - firstly, the disciple is not greater than his teacher, nor the slave greater than his master (Matt. 10:24; Jn. 13:16) Secondly, the disciple or slave is called to be as his teacher or lord (Matt. 10:25).

In Christ's ministry on earth, He performed the works and the greater works of His Father (Jn. 1:50; 5:19-20). The greater works are merely an extension of the works of Christ. The greater works allude to both the quality and excessive number of miracles and healings that will occur in an ascending flow with each believer who trusts God's Word. Like Jesus, believers will do the works and the greater works of Jesus Christ, if they believe. Faith will give us an opportunity to participate in the works that Jesus is doing. The following verses of the opening passage of scripture show us how:

"And whatsoever ye shall ask in my name, that will I do...If ye shall ask anything in my name, I will do it" (Jn. 14:13a-14).

We do the works of Christ by asking in His Name – we ask in His Name, and He does it. In conjunction with asking, the believers are exhorted, by the scriptures, to speak in His Name (Matt. 17:20; 21:21-22; Mk. 11:23-24; Lk. 17:6); to lay hands on the sick in His Name (Mk. 16:18); to command demons to come out in His Name (Mk. 16:17; Ac. 16:16-18); to anoint the sick in His Name (Ja. 5:14-15); and to do whatever needs to be done in His Name to get the sick healed (Col. 3:17). Spirit-filled believers are called to minister to the sick in the same manner that He did, as His representatives and ambassadors on the earth (2 Cor. 5:20).

Jesus gives the basis upon which the greater works ministry operates: "...because I go to the Father" (Jn. 14:12). This basis has a twofold reference - firstly, it alludes to His hour of sacrificial death when He stated that He would go to the Father (Jn. 13:1, 3; 16:5-6, 16-22; Lk. 23:42-43, 46), and secondly, it refers to His resurrection and ascension to the right hand of His Father (Jn. 16:7-13; Mk. 16:20; Ac. 2:32-33). Because Jesus was raised up to sit at the right hand of the Father, we have received the promise of the Spirit to empower us to do the greater works.

The four Gospels and the book of Acts give ample examples of how Jesus and the apostles ministered to the sick and oppressed. These must be the models, patterns, and principles of how the last days Church ought to minister in order to be effective and to get results as they did. The closer we are to the Bible on the topic of healing, the better the results will be.

6

The Healing Ministry of the Believer: Part 2

"And when he had called unto him his twelve disciples, he gave them power against unclean spirits, to cast them out, and to heal all manner of sickness and all manner of disease" (Matt. 10:1).

Jesus Christ, as the Shepherd and Teacher of the twelve apostles, called them to Him and gave them authority and power to preach and to do the works that He did – casting out devils and healing all manner of sickness and disease (Matt. 4:23-24; Lk. 9:1-3). This authority was not only given to the twelve apostles, but it was also given to the seventy other disciples. He commanded them to preach the Kingdom of God and to heal the sick. When they returned from their divine mission, they rejoiced saying that the devils were subject to them through His Name (Lk. 10:1, 9, 17, 19). Then the Lord responded by saying in verse 19,

"Behold I give you power to tread on serpents and scorpions, and over all the power of the enemy: and nothing shall by any means hurt you."

According to the context, Jesus also gave these disciples authority to cast out devils (v17-19) and to heal the sick (v9). The apostles were the prototype of the leadership and the seventy disciples were the prototype of the body ministry – the ministry of the saints (Eph. 4:11-12). These two groups are Christ's blueprint for His "ekklesia", the Church or Assembly of His called-out ones (Matt. 16:18).

After the resurrection of Jesus Christ and just prior to His ascension, He reiterates the preaching and healing ministry of all believers to His disciples saying,

"...Go ye into all the world and preach the gospel to every creature... And these signs shall follow them that believe; In my name shall they cast out devils; ......they shall lay hands on the sick, and they shall recover" (Mk. 16:15, 17, 18).

It is clearly demonstrated from the above verses, that from the mouth of three witnesses, it is concluded that every believer is called to preach the gospel, to cast out devils and to heal every sickness and disease. Every disciple has been given authority to cast out devils and to heal every sickness. This is a work for every believer. That is why the fivefold ministry has been set in the Church, to train and equip the saints for the greater works ministry (Eph. 4:11-13).

The book of James, just like the Gospels, sets forth the healing ministry of the leaders, designated as elders, and that also of believers:

"Is any sick among you? Let him call for the elders of the church; and let them pray over him, anointing him with oil in the name of the Lord: And the prayer of faith shall save [or heal] the sick, and the Lord shall raise him up; and if he have committed sins, they shall be forgiven him. Confess your faults one to another, and pray one for another, that ye may be healed..." (Ja. 5:14-16a).

Here, we can see that healing can be ministered by the elders and the New Testament believers. Elders in leadership minister healing, not because they are elders but because they are believers using their faith to heal the sick. In the above passage of scripture, what makes healing work, is the prayer of faith. Every believer can pray the prayer of faith if they know who they are and what belongs to them. The term "believers" suggests that every one of them have faith. The Apostle Paul writing to the Roman brethren stated,

"For I say through the grace given unto me, to every man that is among you, not to think of himself more highly than he ought to think, but to think soberly according as God hath dealt to EVERY MAN THE MEASURE OF FAITH" (Rom. 12:3).

This verse affirms that every born again Christian has been dealt a measure of faith. It is impossible to be saved, born again, and not have faith for without faith, you could not be saved (Eph. 2:8-9; Rom. 1:17). With that same faith, you can learn to minister healing to the sick without having gifts of healing. Although not every Christian has gifts of healing (1 Cor. 12:30), yet every Christian can minister healing by their faith (Mk. 16:17-18). Galatians 3:5 also testifies to this fact:

"He therefore that ministereth to you the Spirit, and worketh miracles among you, doeth he it by the works of the law, or by the hearing of faith."

If you do not possess gifts of healing, you can manifest healing as a sign and not as a gift (Jn. 14:12).

The term "miracles" in Galatians 3:5 is the Greek plural word "dunameis", meaning "powers". To work supernatural powers stems from the hearing of faith. Hearing the Word of God is how faith comes, and by that faith you are able to work miracles and healings by acting on the Word of God. The bible tells us that faith comes by hearing and hearing by the Word of God (Rom. 10:17). By reading, studying and meditating on the biblical passages of healing, these will cause the faith of God to rise up in you to do these miraculous signs that Jesus promised we could do (Mk. 16:17-18; Jn. 14:12).

Furthermore, every believer has been promised the gift of the Holy Spirit to receive and to minister by faith (Gal. 3:2, 5, 14). The Spirit, who is the source of power within the Spirit-filled believer works through him to perform miraculous signs and wonders. The Holy Spirit is designated as the anointing that abides and remains in the believer forever (Ac. 10:38; Jn. 14:14-15; 1 Jn. 2:20, 27). He does not come and go but remains in the Spirit-filled Christian for fellowship and ministry (Jn. 14:15; Ac. 1:8). And on this basis, the believer can minister healing to the sick any time, any place and anywhere. That healing power ought to be exercised as occasion demands. I will say more about this further in the book.

7

The Hearing of Faith and Healing

"So then faith cometh by hearing and hearing by the word of God" (Rom. 10:17).

Faith is the key that unlocks the supernatural healing power to accomplish what it desires and expects to come to pass (Mk. 11:22-24; Jn. 14:12; Gal. 3:5). If you are going to accomplish anything in the Kingdom of God, it is going to be by faith, for faith is the currency of the Kingdom of God. Without it you cannot please God (Heb. 11:6), neither can you function effectively. So whether you are ministering or receiving healing, faith must be involved.

Faith is believing that God will do for you what He has promised in His Word. Faith, by nature, corresponds to the written Word of God. It only functions in harmony with the Word. The knowledge of the Word is the basis upon which faith operates. Hence the opening passage of scripture - "Faith cometh by hearing and hearing by the word of God" (Rom. 10:17).

The Hearing of Faith and Healing

For this reason there is an inseparable relationship between faith and hearing. If you have not heard, you cannot believe. A person who has never heard the Gospel of Jesus Christ cannot believe in Him. Romans 10:14 affirms,

> How then shall they call on him in whom they have not believed? And how shall they believe in him of whom they have not heard? And how shall they hear without a preacher?"

And on this basis, the apostle writes that faith comes by hearing and hearing by the Word of God (Rom. 10:17).

The Greek rendering for "hearing" is "akoe", which denotes a sense of hearing (1 Cor. 12:17; 2 Peter 2:8). It also signifies a thing heard: a message or teaching. Hence the Greek noun is also translated as "report" in John 12:38 and Romans 10:15. In this regard, the "hearing of faith" can be rephrased, the "message of faith"; the "teaching of faith"; the "report of faith". True biblical faith will not contradict the principles and teachings of the Word of God. It will always be in agreement with Holy Scripture. The more accurate the message, the better the results will be. As you correctly interpret the Word and apply it to your life, the better the faith of God will effectually work in your life. Receiving the unadulterated message of faith will cause faith to work unhindered to produce healing in your own life and in the lives of others (1 Tim. 4:18).

There are two main things that impede the Word of God being fulfilled in us with respect to the ministry of divine healing: firstly, the traditions of men, and secondly, unbelief.

The Traditions of Men

"Howbeit in vain do they worship me teaching for doctrines the commandments of men. For laying aside the commandment of God, ye hold the tradition of men... And he said unto them, Full well ye reject the commandment of God, that ye may keep your own tradition (Mk. 7:7-8a, 9).

The religious leaders made the Word of God of no effect by accepting and practising the teachings of men that contradict the Word of God. Throughout Christendom, there are many teachings that we have accepted and believed which have caused the faith of God and the power of God to become dormant in our lives as it pertains to receiving healing and healing the sick. This has also been true in my own life. These traditions of men are known as "sacred cows" that stop the power of God from operating in our lives. Once these "sacred cows" are unlearned and removed, the healing power of God will begin to flow abundantly and easily in us and through us. These "sacred cows" will be dealt with later on in the book. But for now, the foundational truth is being laid.

According to Romans 10:15, when the unadulterated and uncompromising message or teaching about healing is accepted by faith, then the arm of the Lord will be revealed in all its power to heal and deliver the sick and oppressed (Ac. 10:38). God is waiting on the Church to get its message right concerning divine healing so that His people can be a clear and unblocked channel for God's healing power to be displayed to the world. But before this, the traditions of men that contradict the Word of God concerning healing must be exposed and obliterated from our minds (2 Cor. 10:4-5).

The Hearing of Faith and Healing

UNBELIEF

"Then came the disciples to Jesus apart, and said, Why could not we cast him out? And Jesus said unto them, Because of your unbelief: for verily I say unto you, If ye have faith as a grain of mustard seed, ye shall say unto this mountain, Remove hence to yonder place; and it shall remove, and nothing shall be impossible unto you" (Matt. 17:20).

After Jesus had expelled the demon from the child, thereby healing the boy (v18), His disciples came unto Him and inquired as to why they could not cast the demon out of the child. Jesus' reply was simple: because of their unbelief. It is stated twice in verse 17 and 20 that their unbelief was an hindrance to the boy getting healed. The terms "faithless" (v17) and "unbelief" (v20) are mentioned.

The Greek rendering for these terms are "apistos" (v17) and "apistian" (v20). The word "apistos" means to be unbelieving, untrustworthy, distrustful, unworthy of confidence and belief. This is the perception of a faithless person concerning the living God. They conceive of God to be untrustworthy, not worthy of their confidence and belief. It is a distorted, perverted and twisted view about God. That is why Jesus went on to use the term "perverse" in conjunction with "faithless". The Greek word is "diestrammene", and it literally means to turn aside; to twist or distort.

The disciples could not cast the demon out of the child because their mental belief system became distorted, twisted and turned aside from the straight path, and Jesus made it known that it was because of their unbelief. The Greek word translated "unbelief" is "apistian", and is akin to "apistos", the antithesis of faith and believing. It is also mentioned by Matthew's Gospel in chapter 13:58, where it declares that Jesus could not do any mighty works in his own town because of their unbelief. I will say more about this further in the book, but the important point I want to convey is that unbelief is the result of wrong thinking and ungodly perception. Change your thinking and you will change your perception of God. Having the correct thinking will result in the right understanding that gives birth to true Bible faith (Heb. 11:3).

Jesus' disciples had faith for they left everything to follow Him, for they believed he was the Christ, the Son of the living God. They also performed signs in His Name: healing the sick and casting out devils (Matt. 10:1-8; Mk. 6:7-13; Jn. 18:36-37, 40-41, 45-49; 2:11). What stopped them from helping this demon-possessed boy? The answer was that they allowed unbelief to set in and counteract their faith so that they could not release their faith in God's power to drive out the devil from the boy.

Every believer in Jesus Christ has faith residing in their recreated human spirit (Rom. 12:3; 2 Cor. 4:13), but when you allow unbelief from the world to set into your mind, it will stop the faith of God from rising up in you to defeat that problem. Protect your mind and heart from the unbelieving influences of the world by renewing your mind in the Word of God, so that faith can be activated in you by the acknowledgement of every good thing that is in you, in Christ Jesus (Philm. 1:6). Meditate in prayer and the Word of God so that your mind can understand and agree with your spirit that nothing is impossible to you. It only takes a mustard seed of faith to remove a mountain. The issue is not about how much faith you need to remove mountains; all it takes is faith as the grain of a mustard seed – the smallest of all seeds. Remove the unbelief from your life and let the faith of God flow to touch others.

8

Faith and Healing

"And his name through faith in his name hath made this man strong, whom ye see and know: yea, the faith which is by him hath given him this perfect soundness in the presence of you all" (Ac. 3:16).

Faith plays an essential role in the ministering or receiving of healing from God. Without it, divine healing cannot be given or received. Faith is the means by which the laws of the Kingdom can be tapped into and function for our benefit. Divine healing is a function of the law of the Spirit of life (Rom. 8:2, 11). A law is continuous and consistent like the law of gravity – it is always working. Natural creation is sustained by laws God has established. As it is true in the natural realm, it is even more true in the realm of the spirit, for nature is a reflection of spiritual things. Knowing these laws will enable you to operate them to your advantage and for the glory of God's Kingdom.

The Bible declares that faith is a law that will always work when used by a person to receive anything that they desire from God (Rom. 1:17; 3:27; Matt. 21:22; Mk. 11:23-24).

Faith and Healing

Let us examine the practicalities of how faith operates with respect to healing, and in the meantime destroy some "sacred cows" about faith that pose as an hindrance to its effectiveness in the work of the Kingdom.

The question that needs to be asked is: who needs to have faith for the healing power of God to function and meet the need of the sick? We further need to ask the following: does it require the faith of the one ministering healing; does it necessitate the faith of the one who is sick; does it require the faith of both for the healing power to work?

In Mark's account of the Great Commission in verse 15-18, Jesus first declared the importance of preaching the gospel and the necessity of the sinner to believe in order to be saved:

"...Go ye into all the world, and preach the gospel to every creature. He that believeth and is baptized shall be saved; but he that believeth not shall be damned (v15-16).

So the faith of the recipient is crucial to salvation, but without it the sinner would remain lost. Therefore, the progression is this: the preaching of the gospel will cause faith to come to the sinner who receives the message, and that faith when acted upon will bring salvation to the sinner who believes (Rom. 10:13-15).

In the second part of the Great Commission, miraculous signs performed are solely the responsibility and faith of believers, including the healing of the sick and the deliverance of the demon-possessed. Faith is not necessarily required on their part as sinners or unbelievers. Proof that the sick and demon-possessed are referring to unbelievers is twofold: firstly, the context is about the Great Commission; its purpose is for the lost; to go into the world and preach the gospel to every creature who needs to hear it. The gospel is not for the converted.

Secondly, supernatural signs accompanying the preaching of the gospel are not for Christian believers; they are for unbelievers. For example, one of the litany of signs mentioned, in Mark 16:17, is speaking with new tongues (v16). The Apostle Paul in his letter to the Corinthians confirms that speaking in tongues serves as a sign to unbelievers:

"Wherefore tongues are for a sign, not to them that believe, but to them that believe not..." (14:22a).

Now if tongues is a sign to unbelievers, then all the others signs listed in Mark's Gospel are for the same purpose: signs to unbelievers.

Therefore, deliverance and healing can be ministered to unbelievers by the very fact that believers can exercise faith on their behalf. If there is an exceptional case where sinners exercise faith for healing for themselves or for others, this can be seen in the case of the centurion' servant (Matt. 8:5-13) or the daughter of the Syrophenician woman (Mk. 7:25-30). But if the sinner does not have faith, the Christian believer can have faith for them. That is why in Mark's passage, nothing is mentioned about the sick or demon-possessed having faith for healing or deliverance.

Now regarding a Christian believer who is sick and needs healing, there is a passage of scripture that covers it; and again,

Faith and Healing

the focus is not on the sick having faith for healing, but on the elders praying the prayer of faith to heal the sick.

"Is any sick among you? Let him call for the elders of the church; and let them pray over him, anointing him with oil in the name of the Lord: And the prayer of faith shall save [Gk sozo, heal] the sick, and the Lord shall raise him up; and if he have committed sins, they shall be forgiven him" (Ja. 5:14-15).

The only necessary requirement for the sick to be healed, as it pertains to faith, is for the elders to pray the prayer of faith and the result is: the Lord shall raise him up. It is solely the responsibility of the elders to do this, not the sick. The only responsibility for the sick is to call for the elders of the church. If the sick has faith to be healed, that is commendable, but if he does not, the elders can have faith for him and the Lord will still heal and raise him up.

The sick who calls for the elders does not necessarily mean that the person has faith to be healed. For example, the father of the boy, who had a dumb spirit, came to Jesus' disciples for the boy to be healed, but they could not do it. However, when Jesus came down from the Mount of Transfiguration, the father requested Jesus to heal the boy while he struggled to believe, but Jesus healed the boy anyway by His own faith (Mk. 9:15-27).

The last clause of James 5:15 reads: "...if he have committed sins, they shall be forgiven him." It is interesting to note that the forgiveness of sins is mentioned after the prayer of faith for healing and not before. This passage is teaching us that the sick can be healed before receiving forgiveness. In other words, the sick can be healed while having sin in their lives, the complete opposite of what many have been taught that sin must be removed out of a person's life before they can get healed – this is a tradition of men: "a sacred cow," that is foreign to the Word of God.

In John 5, Jesus healed a man that had an infirmity 38 years, who was waiting at the Pool of Bethesda to be troubled by an angel so that whoever entered first into the water was healed. The only question Jesus asked this man was: "...Wilt thou be made whole?" he did not ask him if he had sin in his life or that he needed to repent of his sin before Jesus would heal. Nowhere in the Gospels did Jesus use repentance or forgiveness of sins as a prerequisite to healing. Jesus just told the impotent man to take up his bed and walk; instantly, he was healed, taking up his bed and walking.

The impotent man did not know who Jesus was when asked by the Jews (v10-13). Then Jesus found the man who was made whole and said,

"...Behold thou art made whole: sin no more, lest a worse thing come unto thee" (v14).

Jesus, after healing the man, pointed out his sin as the root-cause of his infirmity, and commanded him to stop sinning or else a worse thing would come upon him. Sin does not prevent a person from getting healed; it only prevents a person from staying healed (see Lk. 11:24-26). Sin does not stop the recipient from receiving, as long as the person ministering the healing is doing it in faith (Gal. 3:5).

Faith and Healing

There are other scriptural evidences from the ministry of Jesus which shows that one does not have to repent as a condition to receiving healing. On the contrary, the healing ministry of Jesus was a supernatural sign encouraging men to repent and believe the good news of the Kingdom.

Jesus pronounced judgment upon the cities of Chorazin, Bethsaida and Capurnaum because He performed mighty works in these cities and yet, they did not repent. He went on to say that if His mighty works were done in Tyre and Sidon, they would have repented in sackcloth and ashes (Lk. 11:13-15). Although the spiritual climate in Chorazin, Bethsaida and Capurnaum were unrepentant, that did not stop the mighty works of healing being done in these cities (Matt. 11:20-24). It was for this reason Jesus pronounced divine judgment upon them.

If the spiritual climate of these cities did not stop mighty works being done, then how is it that Jesus could not do any mighty work except that he laid hands on a few sick folks and healed them (Mk. 6:5-6)? The Bible went on further to say that Jesus marvelled at their unbelief (v6). Let us examine the nature of their unbelief.

The nature of their unbelief was not that they doubted he could do these mighty works, for they acknowledged that he did them (v2). Neither did they doubt whether they could receive healing by His hands, for the passage does not state it. The nature of their unbelief was that they were offended by Him (v3). They refused to believe that he was the Messiah, the Son of David (Lk. 4:16-18). They dishonoured Him: treated Him with contempt and lightly esteemed Him merely to be the son of Joseph and Mary (v3; Matt. 13:53-58). And for this reason, only a few came to Him to be healed. However, He laid His hands on a few sick folks and everyone of them were healed.

It is so easy to minister healing to the sick that even the nominal Christian with sin in his life will be able to heal the sick, cast out devils, prophesy and still go to Hell. The ungodly Christian will confess these things at the Judgment Seat of Christ, and He will not deny that they did these miraculous signs, but will admit that He never knew them as being saved, for they were workers of iniquity (Matt. 7:21-23). Remember, Judas the betrayer performed healings along with the apostles and still ended up in Hell (Matt. 10:1-8; Mk. 6:7-13). Balaam prophesied blessings by the Spirit concerning Israel and the Messiah and was destroyed with the Midianites because he loved the wages of unrighteousness (Num. 22-24; 2 Peter 2:15-16). Caiaphas, being the high priest that year, prophesied of the death of Jesus Christ and the gathering of the children of God, and then conspired to have Him killed (Jn. 11:49-53). If spiritual gifts can operate through a person having sin in his life, it would also be true of healing because God loves people.

9

Prayer and Healing

"Is any sick among you? Let him call for the elders of the church, and let them pray over him, anointing him with oil in the name of the Lord: And the prayer of faith shall save the sick, and the Lord shall raise him up...Confess your faults one to another and pray one for another, that ye may be. The effectual fervent prayer of a righteous man availeth much" (Ja. 5:14-15ab, 16).

There is a passage in the Book of Acts where Paul entered into a house to pray for the father of Publius, and laying his hands upon him, healed him:

"In the same quarters were possessions of the chief man of the island, whose name was Publius; who received us, and lodged us three days courteously. And it came to pass, that the father of Publius lay sick of a fever and a bloody flux: to whom Paul entered in, and prayed, and laid his hands on him, and healed him" (Ac. 28:7-8).

The verse above states clearly what the Apostle Paul did to minister healing to this sick man; he prayed and laid his hands on him and healed him. Although all these passages tell us to pray for the sick, but they do not inform us about how the sick were prayed for, nor what words were used in the context to pray. However, we can find out how Jesus and the apostles ministered to the sick by looking at examples of how this was done.

The first thing that these New Testament examples teach us about ministering healing is that Jesus and the apostles never asked the Father directly to heal the sick. You will not find one example of it anywhere in the Gospels or the book of Acts. The reason for this is that the apostles and disciples of Christ Jesus were given authority by Christ, over demons, sicknesses and diseases, which culminates in having authority to heal (Matt. 10:1; Mk 6:7; Lk. 9:1-2). Then it reads that Christ commanded them to heal the sick, cleanse the lepers, raise the dead and cast out devils (Matt. 10:8). Notice, the verse did not tell us to pray to the Father to heal the sick or cast out devils, because they were already given the authority to do so. Therefore, what they freely received, they were to freely give. If an employer gives you the authority and the finances to purchase as many chairs as you are able to, would you ask your employer if you could buy chairs? The answer is no! because he has given you authority to do so. In the same vein, Jesus Christ has given the church authority and power to heal the sick, why would we need to pray to Jesus to heal the sick? Jesus, during His earthly ministry, spoke a word of faith to heal the sick and to cast out devils (Matt. 8:16) and He instructed His disciples to do the same thing that he did. When Jesus cursed the fig tree and it was dried up by the roots, He said to His disciples,

Prayer and Healing 55

"...Verily I say unto you, If ye have faith, and doubt not, ye shall not only do this which is done to the fig tree, but also if ye shall say unto this mountain, Be thou removed, and be thou cast into the sea; it shall be done. And all things, whatsoever ye shall ask in prayer, believing, ye shall receive" (Matt. 21:21-22).

Jesus is our model example of how to function in the supernatural power of God. When Jesus cursed the fig tree, he did not do it by praying to the Father to curse the fig tree, but rather, spoke directly to the fig tree saying, "...Let no fruit grow on thee henceforward for ever..." (Matt. 21:19). A simple word of faith spoken to a fig tree, a mountain, a demon or disease will do the impossible, for nothing shall be impossible unto you (Matt. 17:20). All things are possible unto him that believes (Mk. 9:23). This verse shows us how to minister healing to the sick. We are to speak to the mountain to move and not pray to God to move the mountain. He has already given us His authority and His power to move mountains. We have been given authority and power over all sicknesses and devils (Matt. 10:1; Lk. 9:1), so it is your responsibility to command devils to come out and to command sick bodies to be healed. The basic ingredient that will make what you say work, is faith. Jesus said, "If ye have faith, and doubt not...it shall be done" (Matt. 21:21). All that is required is faith as a grain of mustard seed, and NOTHING SHALL BE IMPOSSIBLE UNTO YOU (Matt. 17:20). A mustard seed was the smallest of all seeds in the Middle East. You do not need great faith to remove a great mountain, it only takes faith as a grain of mustard seed (Matt. 17:20; Lk. 17:5-6).

Then Jesus concludes His teaching on faith, saying,

"And all things, whatsoever ye shall ask in prayer, believing, ye shall receive...Therefore I say unto you, What things soever ye desire [Gk ask], when ye pray, believe that ye deceive them, and ye shall have them" (Matt. 21:22; Mk. 11:24).

From these two scriptural passages, Jesus relates what you say to the mountain with what you ask in prayer. After exhorting His disciples to speak in faith to the mountain, He then applies it to praying the prayer of faith and receiving what you asked for. In other words, commanding the mountain to move is attributed to the prayer of petition in the form of a commanding prayer, which is commanding things to change in the Name of Jesus, without commanding God directly. Though the petition is indirect, God is still answering your prayer.

So when the book of James states that "the prayer of faith shall save the sick" (Ja. 5:15), he was referring to a commanding prayer whereby you command the sick person to be healed. Jesus promised that those who believe in the works that He does, they will do those works also (Jn. 14:12). And then the succeeding verses inform us on how these works will be done:

"And whatsoever ye shall ask in my name, that will I do, that the Father may be glorified in the Son. If ye shall ask anything in my name, I will do it" (Jn. 14:13-14).

By commanding things to change through prayer, which is the sense of the above verses, this will cause us to participate with Christ in the miraculous works He is still doing today. Asking in prayer by commanding things to be done in the Name of Jesus will bring about miraculous results.

Prayer and Healing

There are several ways in which you can minister healing to the sick. Firstly, you can command a spirit of infirmity to leave a sick person's body (Matt. 17:18-20; Mk. 9:25). Secondly, speaking a word of healing to the body or a specific part of the body (Matt. 8:2-3; Mk. 7:32-35). Thirdly, you can minister healing merely through the laying on of hands without any words of healing being spoken (Mk. 8:22-25; 16:18). Fourthly, non-medicinal substances were used in the Bible to minister divine healing to the sick such as saliva (Mk. 7:32-35; 8:22-25), the anointed oil (Mk. 6:13; Ja. 5:14), the waters of Jordan, Bethesda and Siloam (2 Kgs. 5:10-14; Jn. 5:1-4; 9:6-7), touching of clothing: a garment, handkerchiefs, and aprons (Mk. 5:27-30; Lk. 6:19; Ac. 19:11-12), a plaister of figs (Is. 38:1-5, 21), the sick looking upon a brazen serpent (Num. 21) and the shadow of Peter healed the sick (Ac. 5). Fifthly, another method of ministering healing was by a word of exhortation or instruction to the sick to do something (2 Kgs. 5:10, 12-14; Mk. 3:5; Lk. 17:13-14). Lastly, healing was ministered by intercessory prayer: asking God to heal a sick person (1 Kgs. 17:18-22).

All these methods were used in Biblical times to heal the sick. But intercessory prayer to God for the sick was never mentioned in the New Testament as a method for healing the infirmed, for Jesus never used it, neither did the apostles or the early church. The methods the Great Physician implemented in His healing ministry did not include prayer - asking His Father to heal the sick, but rather, used the authority He had, to set the captives free. And He is the prime example for every New Covenant believer called into the healing ministry. Jesus' words do not pass away but is continually reverberating in these days,

"...He that believeth on me, the works that I do shall he do also; and greater works than these shall he do, because I go to the Father" (Jn. 14:12).

10

Generational Curses and Divine Healing

"And as Jesus passed by, he saw a man which was blind from his birth. And his disciples asked him, saying, who did sin, this man, or his parents, that he was born blind? Jesus answered, Neither hath this man sinned, nor his parents: but that the works of God should be made manifest in him" (Jn. 9:1-3).

The doctrine of generational curses is being taught in the Body of Christ today. Its basic idea is that the sins of the fathers pass down to their children. In other words, children inherit the consequences of their fathers' sins. This is true in the case of the progenitors of the human race – Adam and Eve – who plunged the human race into darkness and sin. The Bible reads,

"Wherefore, as by one man sin entered into the world, and death by sin; and so death passed upon all men, for that all have sinned" (Rom. 5:12).

As a result of Adam's sin, death came upon all men in three aspects: 1) separation from fellowship with God as the Source of life (Eph. 2:1, 5; Col. 2:13); 2) sickness, disease and infirmity pervaded the human race, also known as incipient death (Rom. 4:19; Heb. 11:12); and 3) physical death and demise by which the life principle, identified as the spirit, is separated from the human body (Gen. 3:19; Ja. 2:26).

This consequence was certain, continuous and inevitable, because of Adam being the federal head of the human race. However, Christ, the head of the redeemed, antitype of the first Adam, undid Adam's sin by bringing life and redemption through His death on the Cross (Col. 1:20; 2:14-15; Heb. 2:14-15). Therefore, through faith in Christ, no born again Christian is legally under any generational curse because Christ has already redeemed us from the curse of the Law (Gal. 3:13-14). We are a new creation in Christ, old things have passed away and behold, all things have become new (2 Cor. 5:17). Our generation no longer goes back to Adam; our generation goes back to Christ and Abraham (Gal. 3:29), and in Christ, there are no generational curses.

Now with respect to the sick, in the ministry of Jesus, His apostles and disciples, not once did any of them have to first deal with a generational curse prior to ministering healing to the sick. There was no confession of the sins of the fathers on the part of the diseased person, or going back into his generations to find out the cause of a physical malady. Even if there were a generational curse behind a physical sickness, all you would need to do is simply heal the sick. No curse or sin can stop it. They all stem back to one source: the oppression of the Devil (Ac. 10:38).

In the opening passage to this chapter, Jesus' disciples inquired whether the blind man or his parents had sinned, that he was born blind. For Jesus, the issue was not whether the blind man

Generational Curses and Divine Healing

sinned, or his parents - a generational curse. But rather, that He should demonstrate the works of God in the man (Jn. 9:1-3). Jesus worked the works of God in him by giving sight to the blind. If there was a generational curse there, it could not stop the power of God from operating in the man's life. If generational curses were not a factor in the ministry of Jesus, it should not be a factor in the healing ministry of the believer (Jn. 14:12). There is no mention of the blind man or anyone else confessing the sins of their fathers before getting healed.

So called teachers of the generational curse doctrine quote certain scriptural passages to support their view: Exodus 20:3-6 reads,

"Thou shalt have no other gods before me. Thou shalt not make unto thee any graven image, or any likeness of any thing that is in heaven above, or that is in the earth beneath, or that is in the water under the earth: Thou shalt not bow down thyself to them, nor serve them: for I the LORD thy God am a jealous God, visiting the iniquity of the fathers upon the children unto the third and fourth generation of them that hate me; And shewing mercy unto thousands of them that love me, and keep my commandments." Other similar passages can be found in Exodus 34:6-7 and Numbers 14:18.

In these passages, it is true that God visits in judgment, the iniquity of the fathers upon the children unto the third and fourth generation. This is true of those who do not know God. However, when the sinner comes in contact with a believer endued with authority, that curse will have to leave at his command without the need of the sinner confessing any generational sins, which is superfluous, as I stated previously. However, if that person does not commit his life to the Lord Jesus Christ, that generational curse will come back on him in some form or other.

With regards to a born again believer, generational curses do not apply, only generational blessings as children of Abraham) Gal. 3:13-14, 29). If a Christian is experiencing symptoms of generational curses, there are three main reasons why this happens: 1) they do not fully understand what Jesus did for us in His sacrificial death on the Cross; 2) they do not have complete comprehension about what it truly means to be born again; and 3) they have been given erroneous teaching about generational curses.

In the sacrificial death of Christ, all curses have been cancelled and blotted out by His blood, whether they be curses written in the Book of the Law (Deut. 27:15-26; 28:15-68) or curses not written therein (Deut. 28:61). The blood of Jesus has cancelled all curses. There two scriptural passages attest to this fact:

"Christ hath redeemed us from the curse of the law, being made a curse for us: for it is written, Cursed is everyone that hangeth on a tree .... Blotting out the handwriting of ordinances that was against us, which was contrary to us, and took it out of the way, nailing it to his cross; And having spoiled principalities and powers, he made a shew of them openly, triumphing over them in it" (Gal. 3:13; Col. 2:14-15).

Christ has delivered us from the curse of the Law; the greek term used for redeemed is "exagorazo", which means to "buy out", and is used especially of purchasing a slave with a view to his freedom. We have been bought out from under the curse of the Law which is death, because Jesus took our place and died on our behalf to free us from the curses that come under the category of death. It is explained in this way since all types of curses are designed to lead to physical demise and destruction (Deut. 28:61; 30:19). The curse that Jesus literally experienced on the Cross was physical death, according to that which was written in the Law (Deut. 21:22-23). The token given to signify His death on the cross is the blood of Jesus Christ. That same blood that justifies and washes away our sins has also removed every single curse including all generational curses. If any one is in Christ, he is a new creation, old things are passed away and all things become new. That means no more demonic oppression or attack on the mind, the emotions or the physical body (3 Jn. 2). You are now a descendant of a blessed bloodline that has no sickness, disease or malady (Gal. 3:13-14, 29). His blood has blotted out the handwriting of ordinances that were against us. And angelic and demonic powers have been plundered at the cross and being made an open exhibition, through the cross, triumphing over them in it.

11

God's Medicine For Divine Healing

"My son, attend unto my words; incline thine ear unto my sayings. Let them not depart from thine eyes; keep them in the midst of thine heart. For they are life unto those that find them, and health to all their flesh" (Prov. 4:20-22).

There is a prescribed remedy for the healing and health of God's people mentioned in the Holy Scriptures. It is the essence of the divine health system in the Kingdom of God – a health package prescribed by the Great Physician. If, for instance, a person was sick, he would go to his physician, and that physician would make a medical diagnosis of his patient, and based on the diagnosis, write out a prescription for a specific kind of medicine that will help cure his sick patient. Similarly, in the realm of the spirit, there is a prescription for God's medicine that will cure every sickness and every disease in humanity. That medicine as prescribed in the opening verses of this chapter, is the Word of God.

As a prescription contains written instruction from a physician as to the type of drug to be given, so the Word of God contains written instructions from the Lord for the application of His Word to our lives for health and healing. There are four specific instructions, from the scriptural passage, that unveil the way to apply God's Word to your physical body (Prov. 4:20-22). The Word of God will heal you like medicine. In verse 22, the term "health" is translated from the Hebrew word "marpe", (pronounced as marpay) and it literally means remedy or medicine. God's Word is medicine to the whole man – spirit, soul and body (1 Thess. 5:23).

The first instruction regarding the application of the Word of God to your life is this: "My son, attend to my words...", that is, give attention to the Word of God. Let it be your priority above all else. Do not give attention to anything else for it will pose as a distraction to you receiving your healing. To attend means to give care to; to be of a ready mind or prepared heart to perform some specific task, and that task is in the next clause of verse 20 - "incline thine ear unto my sayings".

Verse 20 is instructing us to be of a ready mind to hear the Word of God; be prepared and attentive to incline your ears. This does not mean to merely hear with your natural ears but to hear God's Word with your spiritual ears. When you hear with spiritual ears, that means that you understand by revelation of the Spirit. It is possible to hear with the natural ears and yet not understand, because one's spiritual ears are closed. Jesus affirms it by quoting from the Prophet Isaiah,

"Therefore speak I to them in parables: because they seeing see not; and they hearing; hear not, neither do they understand. And in them is fulfilled the prophecy of Esaias, which saith, By hearing ye shall hear, and shall not understand; and seeing ye shall see, and shall not perceive: For this people's heart is waxed gross, and their ears are dull of hearing, and their eyes they have closed; lest at any time, they shall see with their eyes, and hear with their ears, and should understand with their heart, and should be converted, and I should heal them" (Is. 13:13-15).

Seeing with the eyes and hearing with the ears, which are spiritual senses, are a Hebrew parallelism for understanding. In other words, seeing and hearing, are tantamount to understanding, when expressed by the context. Therefore hearing with the spiritual ears always signify that you understand what you are hearing. However, as conveyed by the above scriptural passage, to merely see with the natural eyes and hear with the natural ears will not bring understanding of spiritual things, for the natural man does not receive the things of the Spirit of God for they are foolishness unto him, neither can he know them because they are spiritually discerned) 1 Cor. 2:14). So endeavour always to read the Word of God with spiritual eyes and hear it with spiritual ears. As the physical body has senses, so does the spirit man have senses (Heb. 5:14).

When the scriptural passage exhorts us to incline our ears unto his sayings (Prov. 4:20), it is instructing us to understand what we have inclined our ears unto. Do not be like the Israelites who heard the Word preached, but it did not profit them because the Word was not mixed with faith in those who heard it (Heb. 4:2). Faith is the means by which we understand truth (Heb. 11:3). If there is no understanding, it is because there is no faith applied to the Word of God. Faith and understanding imply that the Word of God is planted deep within the soil of one's heart (Matt. 13:18-19). To nurture a heart of understanding, you must spent time prayerfully meditating on the Word that you have studied

(Josh. 1:8; 1 Tim. 4:15). Meditation will translate information into revelation. The Apostle Paul confirms this by saying,

"Consider what I say; and the Lord give thee understanding in all things" (2 Tim. 2:7).

The word "consider", also means to meditate. For God's medicine – the Word of God, to work in your life and body, you must meditate, ponder and consider the scriptural verses on healing; and in doing so you will understand, be converted and the Lord will heal you, as spoken in the prophecy of Isaiah (Matt. 13:15).

The next clause of verse 21 states, "Let them not depart from thine eyes...". Notice how this verse comes after hearing words. Hearing the Word of God will consequently create a vision or picture that corresponds to the words heard previously - words form pictures. The verse does have a reference of reading the Word with your eyes, but its deeper meaning applies to having a vision of the Word concerning your health as well as everything promised to you in God's Word. His Word is described as a mirror in 2 Corinthians 3:18,

"But we all, with open face beholding as in a glass the glory of the Lord, are changed into the same image from glory to glory, even as by the Spirit of the Lord."

The Greek term for "glass" here is "katoptrizo", which signifies a mirror. When the veil of sin, traditions and unscriptural biases are removed, we are able to see with unveiled face the glory of the Lord – His image, nature, character and excellence – and are metamorphosed into the same image that we behold in the Word of God. Do not merely hear the Word but see its glory –

behold the glory of divine health for that is what you have become; "...by whose stripes ye were healed" (1 Peter 2:24).

Just as you are the righteousness of God, you are also the healed of God. The Word of God is a mirror that reflects who you are in the realm of the Spirit, irrespective of your circumstances. Your true identity is in the Word. You are the glory of the Lord by virtue of your union with Him (1 Cor. 6:17). The Word of God gives a reflection of who you are in Christ, and in Him, you are already healed (1 Peter 2:24). You are no longer the sick.

An aspect of the glory of God is divine health for it is the expression of the life of God. He cannot get sick because He is life itself. The same glory that raised Jesus from the dead will also make alive your mortal body (Rom. 6:4; 8:11). We, who are born again, are here on this earth to reflect God's glory. The verbal form of glory is "glorify," and we are told to glorify God in our bodies and in our spirits which are God's (1 Cor. 6:20). God is glorified in your body when it is well. See yourself well in God's Word and you will experience His life in your body.

The next clause of verse 21 instructs us to "...keep them in the midst of thine heart". Keeping God's words in the midst of your heart indicates that you have not only understood them but also have apprehended the very things that His words communicate. When we understand His Word, we possess by faith the things that belong to us in Christ (Mk. 11:24; Heb. 11:1) and therefore will be manifested in our lives. But what we desire must be seized, obtained and apprehended in our spirit before we can physically enjoy the things which God has freely given to us.

This is completely true of healing. It must be true reality in your heart, succeeded by the physical manifestation, and you do this by spending time meditating in the Word of God. The faith to obtain comes by hearing the Word of God (Rom. 10:17). As a result of following God's instructions, His Word will be life to those who find it and health to all your flesh (v22). It reads,

"For they are life unto those that find them, and health to all their flesh."

Giving attention to God's Word will produce healing in your body. Keeping His Word in your heart will cause you to walk in divine health (Ex. 15:26; 23:25-26; Deut. 7:13-15). You may get healed by the faith of someone else. But if you do not apply His Word to your life on a daily basis, the same sickness, or something else will come upon you. Divine health is better than divine healing. It is God's best for the child of God. To live in divine health, 3 John 1:2 informs us that divine health is obtained by prospering the soul. To the degree that you prosper in your soul is to the extent that you will walk in divine health.

How do you prosper in your soul? You prosper in your soul by following the instructions laid in Proverbs 4:29-22; and then verse 23 exhorts us,

"Keep thy heart with all diligence: for out of it are the issues of life."

All diligence need to be applied to guarding your heart in order to obtain divine health in all your flesh – that is perfect health.

The above verse shows us that divine health begins on the inside – the heart – and works itself out, for from the heart are the issues of life. The Amplified Bible defines the issues of life as "...flows springs of life." Out of the regenerated heart of a Christian flows the forces of life. Your heart will determine the course or direction of your life. As the heart goes, the person will follow. Therefore, do not allow anything that is contrary to the life of God in you to enter your heart. Keep the life of God flowing in your heart for it will determine the outcome of your life. Nurture the life of God in you by meditating on the Word of God and you will live in divine health. Keep the wellsprings of life flowing through the words of your mouth on a daily basis (Prov. 18:4). Do not allow sickness, disease or death of any kind proceed out of your mouth as unbelief, for that will impede the divine flow of the life of God.

12

Paul's Thorn in the Flesh

"And lest I should be exalted above measure through the abundance of the revelations, there was given to me a thorn in the flesh, a messenger of Satan to buffet me, lest I should be exalted above measure. For this thing I besought the Lord thrice, that it should depart from me. And he said unto me, My grace is sufficient for thee: for my strength is made perfect in weakness. Most gladly therefore will I rather glory in mine infirmities, that the power of Christ may rest upon me. Therefore I take pleasure in infirmities, in reproaches, in necessities, in persecutions, in distresses for Christ's sake: for when I am weak, then am I strong" (2 Cor. 12:7-10).

This passage has been taught that God puts sickness and disease on His children to keep them humble. Is that what this passage is actually saying? Or did Paul have a physical infirmity such as an eye problem or ailment? The purpose of this chapter is to explore whether this premise is doctrinally correct or whether it is a man-made tradition unsupported in Scripture - one of the sacred cows that need to be exposed as erroneous. This text will be examined in its context and co-text to arrive at the correct biblical interpretation. In aligning myself to the quote from a Jewish Bible teacher, who declared, "A text out of context in isolation from its co-text is unmistakeably the signature of Satan", I will endeavour to approach this subject from its text, context and co-text to arrive at its correct biblical conclusion.

In context, the Apostle Paul stated at the outset of 1 Corinthians 12 that it was not profitable for him to glory because of the visions and revelations he experienced of the Lord. Therefore, he decided not to glory or boast concerning the abundance of visions and revelations of the Lord but rather to glory in the things that concern His infirmities (v1, 5). This exaltation through the abundance of the revelations was deemed as unprofitable for him (v1), foolish (v6) and above measure in people's estimation of him. God desires His people to be exalted (1 Peter 5:6; Matt. 23:12) but not exalted above measure in your own estimation of yourself or in others opinion of you (2 Cor. 12:6). Apostle Paul admonished the saints:

"...not to think of himself more highly than he ought to think; but to think soberly..." (Rom. 12:3).

However, according to the passage, the concern was not about the Apostle Paul exalting himself but rather others exalting him above measure because of the abundant revelations and for this reason, he retrained himself to rejoice or glory in them (2 Cor. 12:5). So instead he would glory in his infirmities.

The apostle intimates one of his visionary revelations, speaking of himself in the third person, as one who was caught up to paradise in the third heaven and heard things that were unlawful to utter (v2-4). A certain hint that this man, caught up to heaven, was the Apostle Paul was implied in the fact that he could not

Paul's Thorn in the Flesh

tell whether his experience was in the body or out of the body, thus concluding that God alone knew (v2-3).

The Greek term for "glory" is "kauchaomai", which means to boast or rejoice" and this is done through announcement or proclamation with the tongue. In this chapter, Paul does not directly or clearly announce that the man was him, neither does he go into detail about his visionary revelation. But he does go into detail about his infirmities and sufferings in the preceding chapter (2 Cor. 11:23-33).

Now the purpose of the Apostle being given a thorn in the flesh, was so that others would not think of him above that which they could see him to be (v5). The first point where men's tradition gets it wrong is that they say that Paul was given a thorn in the flesh to keep him humble. In fact, the scriptural passage does not actually state that. It was not given for Paul's sake but rather the sake of others, so that they do not exalt him above measure in their estimation of him (v5-6).

Now, we come to the heart of this chapter: what was Paul's thorn in the flesh? Let me begin by stating what the verse actually says. The Apostle Paul declares, in verse 7, "...there was given to me a thorn in the flesh, the messenger of Satan to buffet me, lest I should be exalted above measure." The passage actually says that the thorn in the flesh was a messenger of Satan. In the Greek rendering of "angelos", the translation of the word is better rendered "angel"; so the phrase should be read, "angel of Satan". Therefore, thorn in the flesh is not literal, but is used metaphorically to refer to a supernatural personality sent by Satan to buffet the apostle. To buffet, in the Greek, means to strike with clenched hands, the purpose of which is to inflict injury, damage, harm or pain.

The Apostle who was a scholar of the Old Testament Scriptures, used a term or synonym that was also employed by biblical characters and authors to convey the same idea. For example, during Israel's conquest of Canaan, they did not obey God's voice to destroy the nations that were in the land, but made covenants for them to pay tribute to Israel. So an angel of the lord came up from Gilgal unto Bochim saying,

"And ye shall make no league with the inhabitants of this land; ye shall throw down their altars: but ye have not obeyed my voice; why have ye done this? Wherefore I also said, I will not drive them out from before you; but they shall be as thorns in your sides, and their gods shall be a snare unto you" (Judg. 2:2-3).

In Israel's history, especially during the period of the judges, they were ensnared and enticed to worship the gods of the nations in Canaan. God sent the nations, whose gods they worshipped, against them to oppress, mistreat and harm, and Israel served their oppressors until they cried unto the Lord to deliver them Judg. 3). It is in this sense that the nations became as thorns in Israel's side – a metaphor alluding to the fact of the nations oppressing, injuring, harming mistreating and persecuting Israel when enticed to commit idolatry.

The scriptural passage previously mentioned is a reiteration and fulfilment of the prophetic words spoken by Joshua after the Lord had given Israel rest from her enemies, and it reads,

"Else if ye do in any wise go back, and cleave unto the remnant of these nations, even these that remain among you, and shall make marriages with them, and go in unto them, and they to you: Know for a certainty that the LORD your God will no more drive out any of these nations from before you; but they shall be snares and traps unto you, and scourges in your sides, and thorns in your eyes, until ye perish from off this good land which the LORD your God hath given you" (Josh. 23:12-13).

God warned Israel, through Joshua, not to become unequally yoked with the nations of Canaan and not to make marriages with them, or else they would become ensnared by their idolatrous practices. Such practices would eventually lead to the very nations with which they entered into covenant, turning against them to become scourges in their sides and thorns in their eyes. In other words, God would use them as a rod of chastisement against Israel to persecute them, cause distress and destroy them until they perish from the land. And so this was fulfilled in the time of the judges when they turned away from God's commandments.

There is nowhere in these two passages that any reference is made to sickness or disease. The metaphoric terms such as "thorns", "scourges", "pricks", are merely figures of Israel being afflicted, tormented, persecuted and harmed by their national enemies. Similarly, the Apostle Paul's thorn in the flesh was an angel of Satan, an enemy of the Gospel, to buffet him. How he was to suffer was indicated in his conversion and calling when the Lord spoke to Ananias concerning him:

"For I will shew him how great things he must suffer for my name's sake" (Ac. 9:16).

The Lord informed Ananias that Paul would suffer great things for His Name's sake. The nature of this suffering was described by Jesus' teaching in the Sermon on the Mount:

"Blessed are ye when men shall revile you, and persecute you, and shall say all manner of evil against you falsely, for my sake" (Matt. 5:11).

Firstly, Paul's suffering was for His Name sake. Every time suffering for His Name sake is mentioned, it is referring to being persecuted, reviled, being accused falsely or hated and mistreated for representing Christ in your preaching, teaching or manner of life. Suffering for His Name sake never alludes to sickness or disease, which Jesus Christ bore away on the Cross (Is. 53:4-5; Matt. 8:16-17). The only logical explanation is persecution. Paul's use of the term "infirmities", must always be looked at in context. All sicknesses, diseases and physical disabilities are designated as infirmities or weaknesses (Matt. 8:16-17; Lk. 8:2; 13:8), but not all infirmities are physical disabilities, sicknesses and diseases. There are infirmities that are called temptations (Heb. 4:15); spiritual and moral weakness (Heb. 5:2-3); ignorance (Rom. 8:26); mortal death itself (1 Cor. 15:43b); the physical sufferings and death of Jesus Christ on the cross, and the persecutions, temptations and sufferings of the Apostle Paul and his fellow-ministers in Christ (2 Cor. 13:4).

The Apostle Paul suffered more than all the apostles because of this angel of Satan who stirred up persecution in places that he went to preach the Gospel. In Chapter 11 of 2 Corinthians, he lists the things that happened to him, and then conclude by calling those things his infirmities, of which he will glory in (2 Cor. 11:24-

30). There is no mention in that list of Paul suffering sickness, disease or a physical disability that impeded him in the work of the gospel. He lived in supernatural strength and health by the Spirit who lived in him (Rom. 8:11).

Bibliography

Harris, R. Laird et al (1980), "Theological Wordbook of the Old Testament" Vol 1 & 2. Chicago: Moody Press.

Vine, W E (1985), "An Expository Dictionary of Biblical Words." Chicago: Moody Press.

www.ingramcontent.com/pod-product-compliance
Lightning Source LLC
Chambersburg PA
CBHW050445010526
44118CB00013B/1686